Bible Stories to Draw and Tell

Bible Stories to Draw and Tell

Julie A. Petras

Our Sunday Visitor Publishing Division
Our Sunday Visitor, Inc.
Huntington, Indiana 46750

Write:
Our Sunday Visitor Publishing Division
Our Sunday Visitor, Inc.
200 Noll Plaza
Huntington, IN 46750

ISBN: 1-931709-39-4
(Inventory No. R24)

Illustrations by Julie A. Petras
Cover and interior design by Tyler Ottinger

PRINTED IN THE UNITED STATES OF AMERICA

Table of Contents

How to Use This Book

- Highlight the word(s) and corresponding lines to be drawn.
- The storyteller draws a line or two as the story is told.
- Practice drawing and telling/reading the story several times before presenting it to the children.
- Change the wording to fit the age group.
- Draw on paper.
    - The finished drawing can be given to the child who identifies the picture.
- Have the children "keep the secret" until the end of the story even if they think they can identify the picture.
- Younger children generally enjoy watching and listening as the story is read/told.
- Older children might enjoy drawing along with the storyteller or writing and drawing their own.

And It Was Good

A Creation Story

(Based on Genesis 1:1 to 2:2-3)

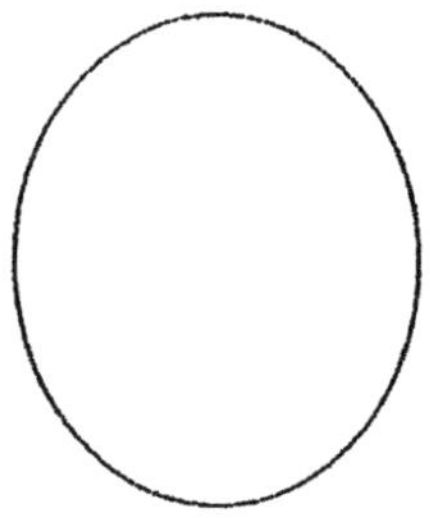

A long, long, long time ago there was nothing, nothing except **GOD**.

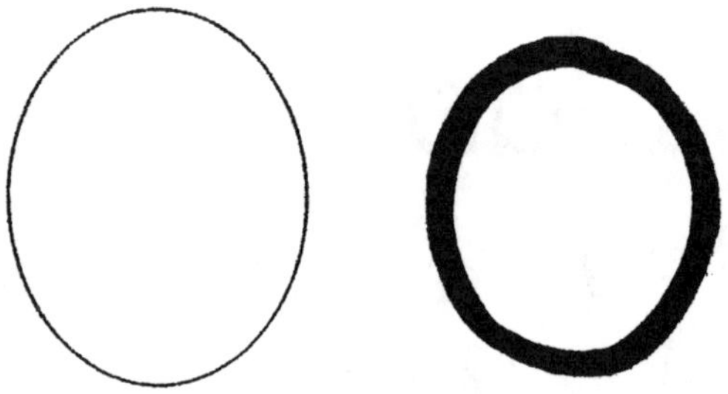

One day God said to Himself, "I think I'll create some things." On the first day God said, "Let there be **LIGHT**," and there was. And God said it was "Good."

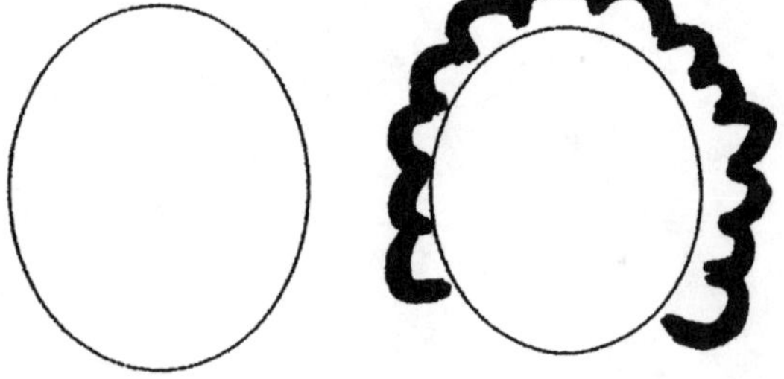

On the second day God said, "Let there be a **SKY**," and there was. And God said it was "Good."

On the third day God said,
"Let the **LAND** be here ...

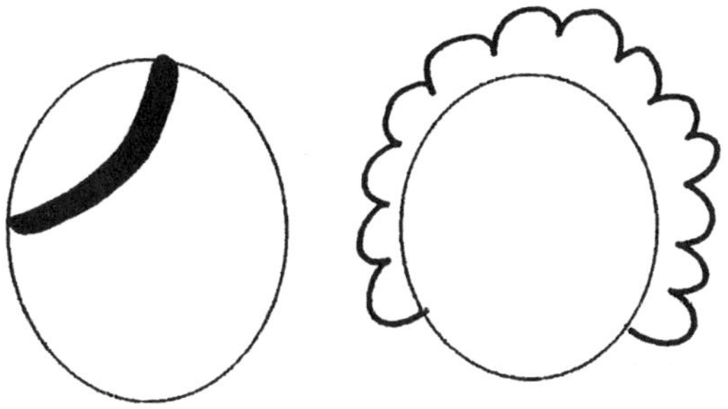

... and let the **SEA** be there,"
and it was. And God said it
was "Good."

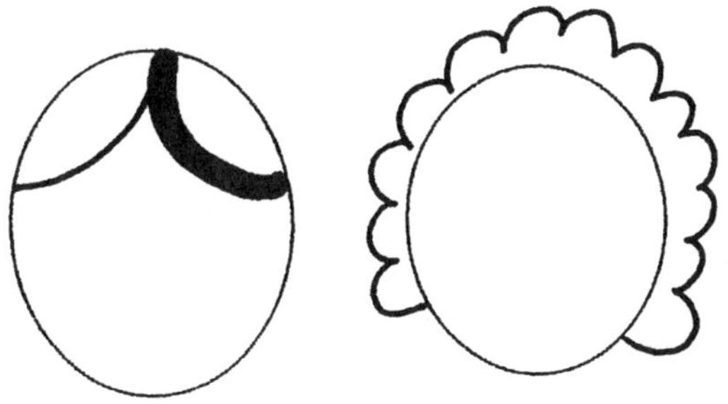

Then God put **PLANTS** ...

... and **TREES** all over the land. And God said it was "Good."

On the fourth day God said, "Let there be lights in the sky." God created the **SUN** ...

... and the **MOON**. And God said it was "Good."

On the fifth day God said, "Let there be **FISH** in the sea …

… and **BIRDS** in the air," and there were. And God said it was "Good."

On the sixth day God said, "Let there be **ANIMALS** all over the land," and there were.

Then God said, "I want to create something really special.
Something more like me."
So God created again.

What do you think God made?
(People.)

And God said it was "Great!"

On the seventh day God took a rest.

A Man Named Noah

(Based on Genesis 6:5 to 9:17)

A long, long time ago many people in the world did not do what God wanted. There was only one man and his family who were **VERY GOOD**. His name was Noah.

God told Noah to build **A BIG BOAT** called an ark.

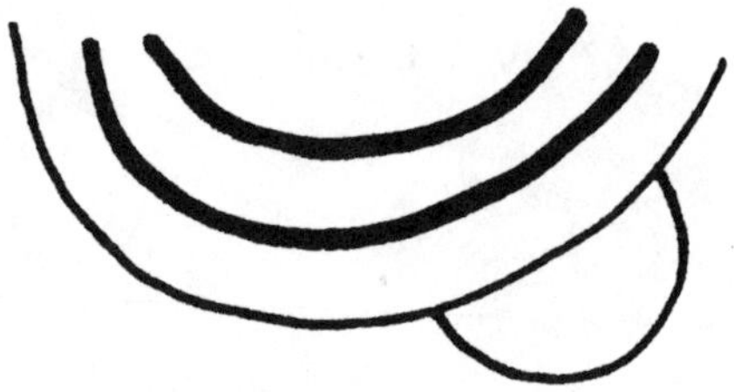

Then God told Noah to fill the ark with two of every kind of animal. So Noah found ...

ONE-TWO GIRAFFES

TWO SNAKES

ONE-TWO ELEPHANTS

TWO KANGAROOS

TWO CAMELS

TWO BEARS

TWO HORSES

TWO ZEBRAS

When all the animals, Noah, and his family were in the ark, it started to rain. It **RAINED**, and it **RAINED**, and it **RAINED** — for forty days and forty nights.

When the rain finally stopped and the land was dry again, Noah and his family left the ark. They thanked God for saving them from the flood. God put a special sign in the sky to show Noah His promise never to send a big flood again.

What sign did God put in the sky?
(A rainbow.)

Abraham

(Based on Genesis 12-21)

Abram and his wife, Sarai, were shepherds. They were nomads who wandered from **PLACE to PLACE**.

They were very old. They had many **SHEEP** and ...

... many **POSSESSIONS** but no children.

One day **GOD** spoke to Abram.

God told him to **LEAVE** the country where he was and go to a place that God would show him.

Abram and Sarai **LEFT** and **WENT** to the land called Canaan.

God changed Abram's name to Abraham and promised him he would have many descendants.

God told Abraham to count **ALL THE STARS** in the sky. He said that the people in Abraham's family would someday number more than all of these stars.

Abraham's wife finally had a baby boy. They named him Isaac.

What did Abraham live in as he moved from place to place? (A tent.)

Rebekah

(Based on Genesis 24:1 to 25:26)

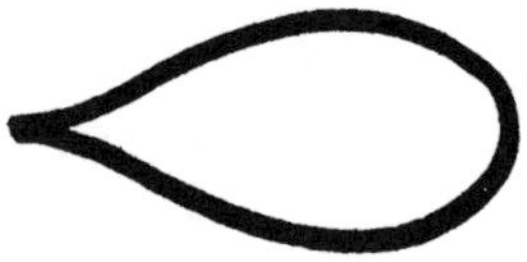

Abraham's son **ISAAC** wanted to get married and have a wife.

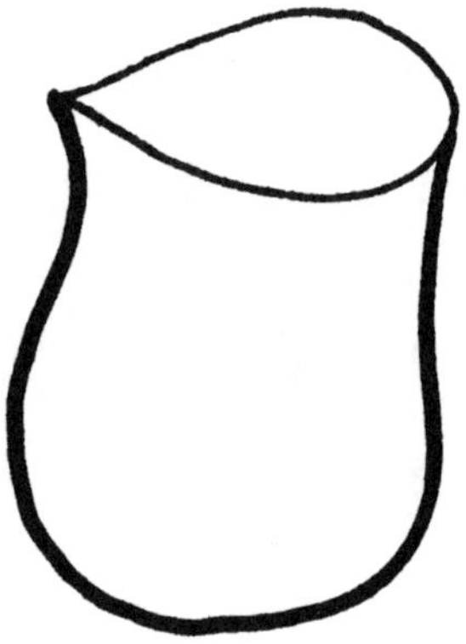

Abraham sent his **SERVANT**, a man who worked for him, out to find someone for Isaac to marry.

After traveling for a while he was **HOT** ...

… and **TIRED**, so he stopped to rest near a well.

A girl named **REBEKAH** was nearby.

She offered to get the servant a **DRINK** from the well.

She also got something for the **CAMELS** to drink.

The servant thought that Rebekah would be a good wife for Isaac. When she and Isaac got married, she had **TWIN SONS**.

They named them **JACOB** and **ESAU**.

What did Rebekah use to get the water from the well? (A pitcher.)

Joseph, Son of Jacob

(Based on Genesis 37:1-3, 12-28, Genesis 42-45)

A man named **JACOB** had twelve sons.

His favorite son was named **JOSEPH**.

Jacob gave Joseph a **SPECIAL GIFT**.

When his **BROTHERS** saw this, they were jealous. They wished their father had given them something.

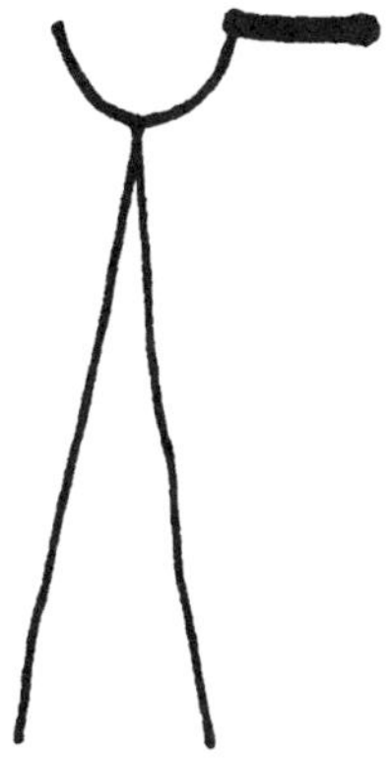

One day when he was still very **FAR AWAY**, his brothers saw Joseph coming toward them and they decided to get rid of him.

When he got close, his brothers **GRABBED** him and threw him **DOWN INTO A DEEP DRY WELL**.

After a while they saw some men **GOING TO THE LAND OF EGYPT**. His brothers sold Joseph to the men to be their slave.

After many years Joseph **WAS FREED** and he became an important man in Egypt.

MANY MORE YEARS PASSED. His brothers came to Egypt because they needed food.

Joseph **RECOGNIZED HIS BROTHERS**.

He forgave them and gave them **ALL THE FOOD** they needed.
(Use different colors.)

Joseph, his father, Jacob, his brothers, and all their families came to live together in Egypt. Joseph had forgiven them for what they did to him and they were no longer jealous of him.

What did Joseph's father give to him?
(A coat.)

Clip Notes

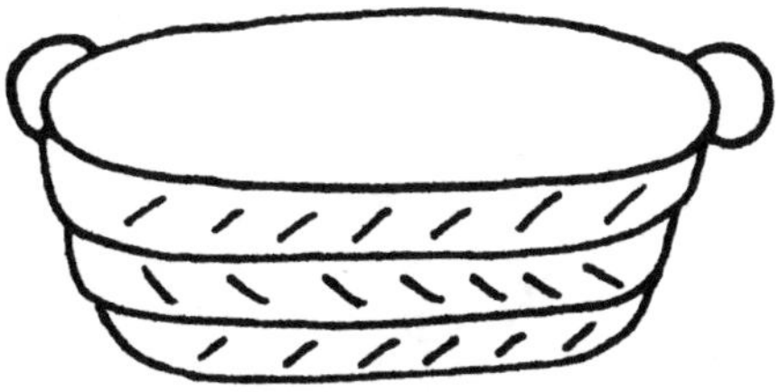

Moses

(Based on Exodus 2:1-6)

There was a time when God's special people, the **ISRAELITES**, were forced to work as slaves in the country called Egypt.

The **KING**①, who was called a Pharaoh, made them work **VERY HARD**②.

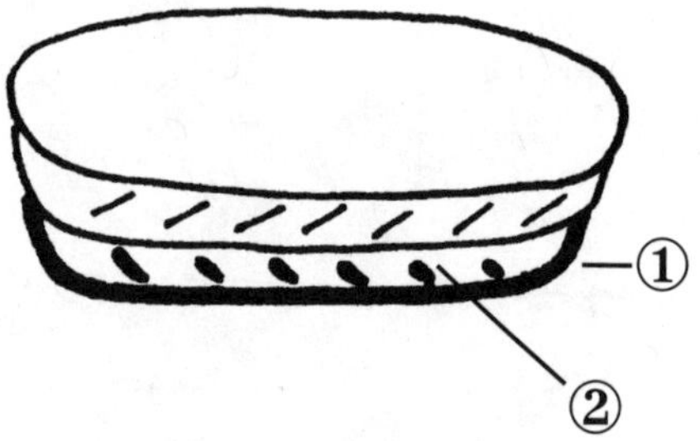

They had to take **STRAW**① and ...
... mix it with mud and make it into **BRICKS**②.

One day the **PHARAOH** decided to punish the Israelites even more.

He told his soldiers to go out and take all the **LITTLE BABY BOYS** away from their homes.

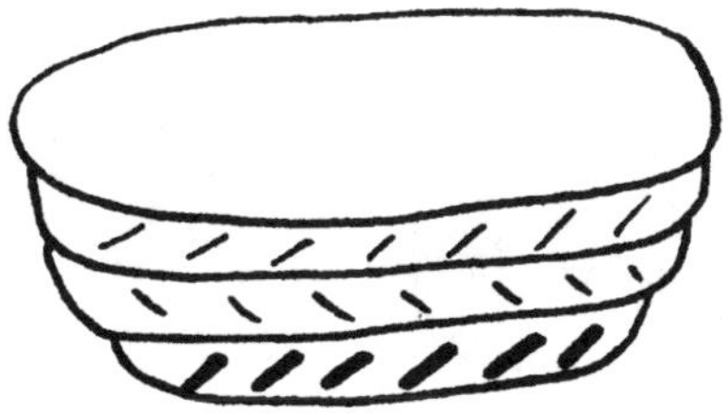

One **MOTHER** wanted to save her son, Moses, from the soldiers.

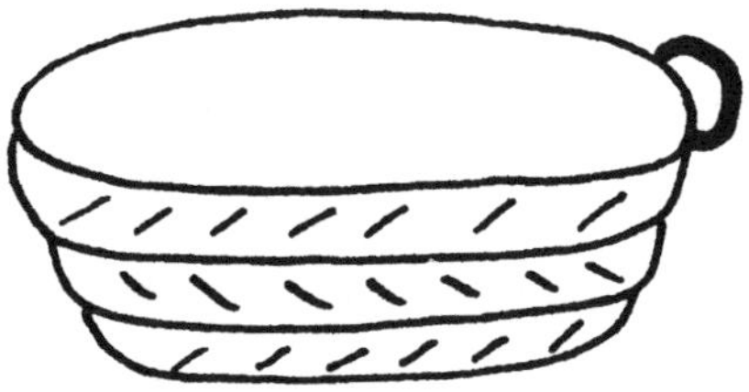

She wrapped him in a blanket, made a little boat, placed him in it, and put the boat in the river.

The little boat carried Moses safely down the river. The Pharaoh's **DAUGHTER** was near the river that day.

She was so happy to find the baby that she took him home to the palace and took care of him as her own son.

What did Moses' mother use as a boat for the baby?
(A basket.)

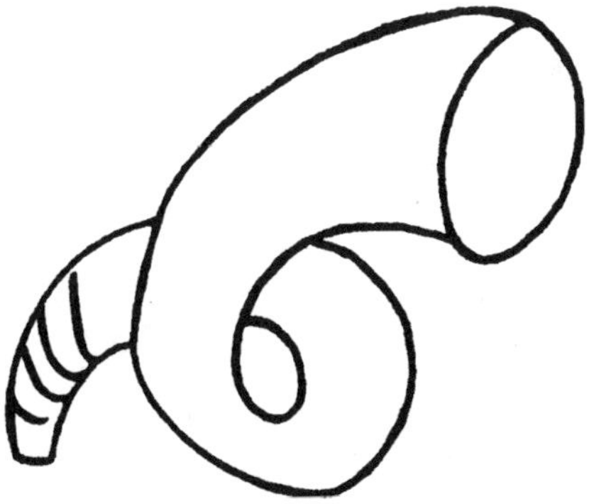

Joshua and the Battle of Jericho

(Based on Joshua 3:14-17, 6:1-20)

Joshua became the leader of God's people, the Israelites, after **MOSES** died.

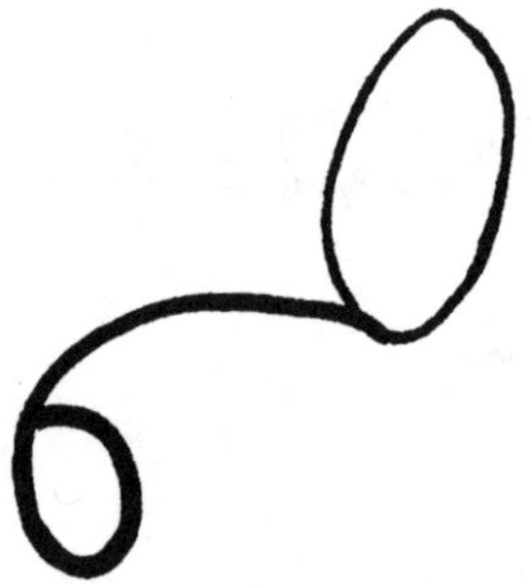

He led the people to the **JORDAN RIVER**.

As they carried the **ARK OF THE COVENANT** into the river, the river dried up so that all the people could cross on dry land.

When they reached the **WALLED CITY** of Jericho, God told Joshua how to conquer it.

They **MARCHED AROUND THE CITY** in silence for six days.

On the seventh day they shouted and blew an instrument to make a lot of noise.

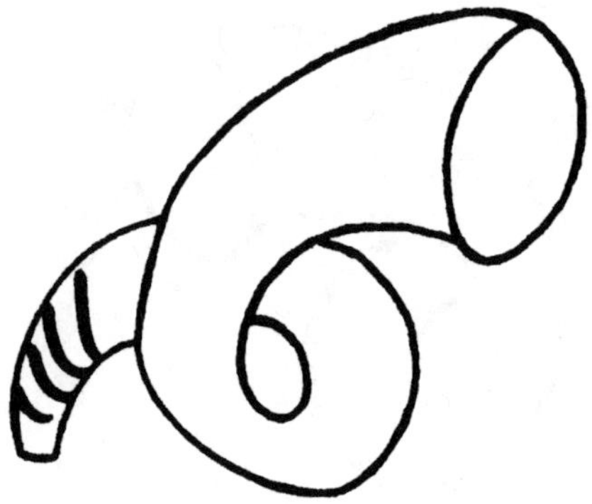

The walls shook and shook and finally fell down. Joshua and **ALL THE ISRAELITES** entered the city.

What did they blow to make the noise?
(A horn. [Explain ram's horn.])

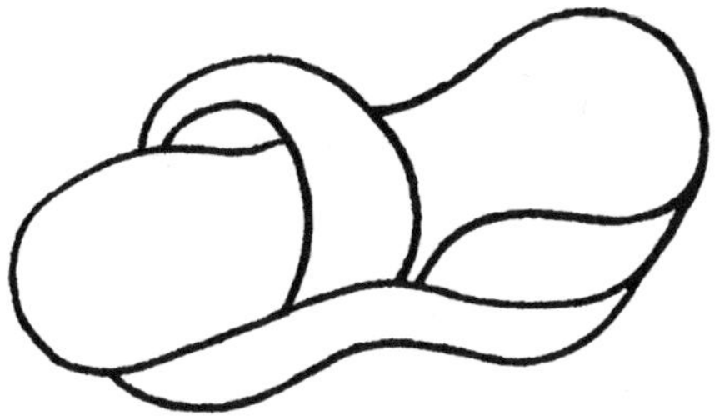

Ruth

(Based on Ruth 1:1-18, 2:1-7,4)

A long time ago there was a woman named **NAOMI**.

She lived in the land of **MOAB**.

Naomi's husband was dead, but she had **TWO SONS**.

EACH OF HER SONS was married.

When her sons died, Naomi decided to go back home to the city called **BETHLEHEM**.

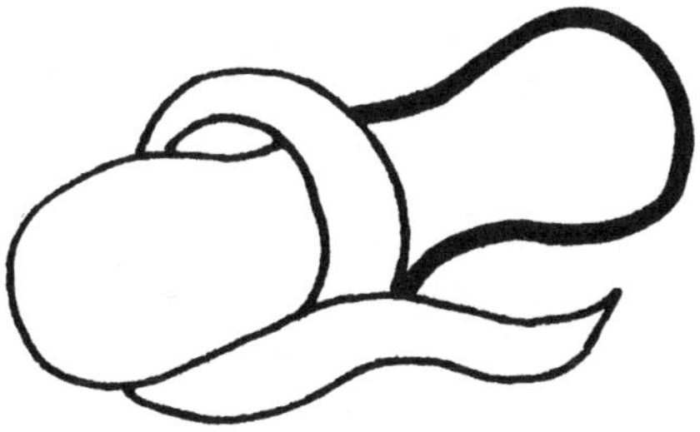

One of her sons' wives, Ruth, insisted on going with Naomi to help and take care of her. She said, "Wherever you go I will go. Your people will be my people."

They were very poor, so when they got to Bethlehem, Ruth went to work in the **FIELDS** of a man named Boaz. Boaz and Ruth fell in love and got married. They stayed in Bethlehem and took care of Naomi. Ruth became an ancestor of Jesus.

What did Ruth wear as she walked with Naomi?
(Shoes.)

David, a Shepherd Boy

(Based on 1 Samuel 16:14-23, 17:1-51)

A long time ago there was a man named Jesse who had **EIGHT SONS**.

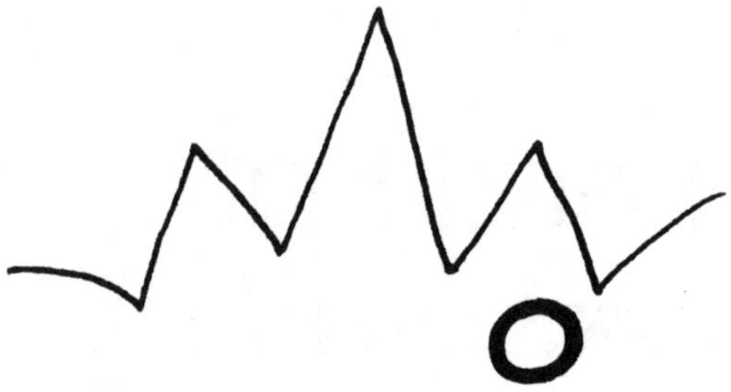

The youngest son was David. David was a shepherd, who took care of his **SHEEP**.

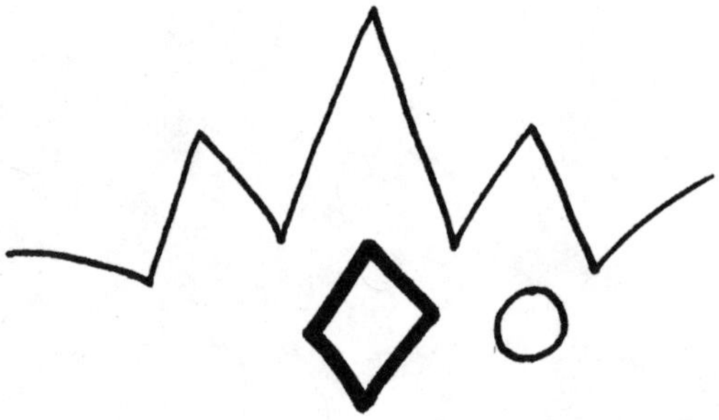

While David watched over his sheep, he played the **HARP** and wrote beautiful songs.

One day King Saul asked David to **COME AND PLAY** for his soldiers who were fighting against the Philistines. King Saul thought David's song would cheer up his men.

The leader of the Philistines decided that one of their soldiers, a very **TALL MAN** named Goliath, should fight one of King Saul's men.

DAVID talked King Saul into letting him fight Goliath.

Goliath laughed when he saw the boy David come out to fight him. But God helped David. David picked up a small **STONE**, put it into his slingshot, and swung it around his head.

With God's help the stone flew straight and hard and hit Goliath in the head. Goliath was defeated!

When David grew up, God had a very special job for him. This is what David wore.

What job did God give David?
(King.)

King Solomon

(Based on 1 Kings 1, 3, 5-7)

King David had a son named **SOLOMON**.

Before King David **DIED**, he told Solomon that to be a great king, he should be faithful to God and love Him with all his heart and soul.

After Solomon became king, God said he could ask for **ANYTHING** and God would give it to him.

Solomon asked God to make him **WISE** so that he would be a good **KING**.

God was pleased because Solomon did not ask for **MONEY** or anything for himself.

Solomon soon became famous because he was such a good, **WISE** king.

God wanted Solomon to build something special for Him. Solomon got the best **STONE**, **GOLD**, and **JEWELS** from all over the country.

He sent men to a country called Lebanon to cut the finest **CEDAR TREES** available.

It took seven years and a lot of hard work, but finally it was complete.

What did Solomon build to honor God?
(A temple.)

Daniel

(Based on Daniel 6:2-25)

Once there was a king named **DARIUS**.

King Darius knew a man named **DANIEL**.

There were **SOME MEN** who did not like Daniel.

These men tricked King Darius into making a law that said everyone must bow down and **PRAY** to the king.

Daniel knew that this was wrong and he would only pray to **GOD**.

The men heard about this and told the **KING**.

King Darius knew he had been tricked, but a law is a law, so he had Daniel **LOCKED UP** with some very mean animals.

King Darius hoped that Daniel would be safe from the animals during the night. Daniel spent the night talking to God. He **PRAYED** and **PRAYED** and **PRAYED**.

In the morning King Darius went to see Daniel. He was **ALL RIGHT**. God had saved Daniel from the animals.

King Darius was happy that Daniel was saved. He punished the men who had tricked him.

From what kind of animals did God save Daniel?
(Lion.)

Clip Notes

Jonah

(Based on Jonah 1-3)

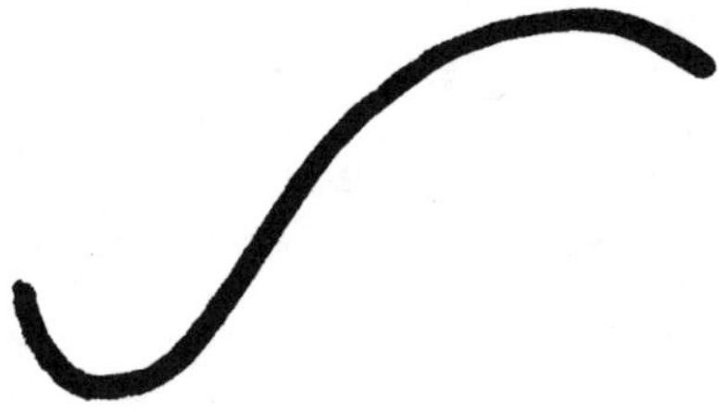

Once there was a man named Jonah. Here's a "**J**" for Jonah's name.

One day **GOD SPOKE TO JONAH**.

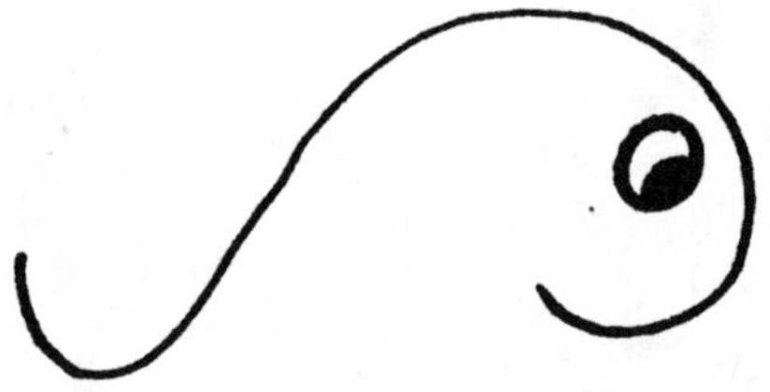

God wanted Jonah **TO GO TO THE CITY OF NINEVEH** to tell the people there that they were not behaving as God wanted them.

Jonah didn't want to go to Nineveh, so he got on a boat **THAT WAS GOING THE OTHER WAY**.

Jonah **TRIED TO HIDE** from God.

While Jonah was on the boat, **GOD SENT A BIG STORM**.

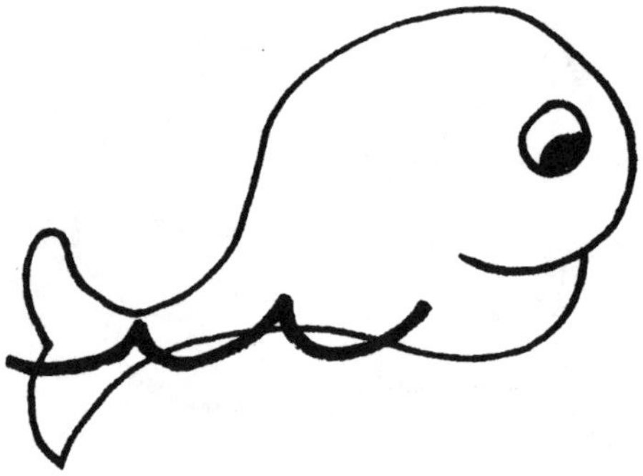

The waves got **HIGHER AND HIGHER** and rocked the boat.

Jonah knew God was angry with him and he told the sailors to **THROW HIM OVERBOARD**.

But Jonah didn't drown. God sent A **BIG ANIMAL** to swallow Jonah.

Jonah stayed inside the animal's belly for **ONE-TWO-THREE DAYS**.

Inside, Jonah prayed and told God he was sorry. Then the animal **SPIT** Jonah out and he landed in Nineveh.

Jonah finally did as God wanted. He talked to the people in Nineveh.

What animal saved Jonah?
(A whale.)

Clip Notes

A Message from God

The Annunciation
(Based on Luke 1:26-38)

A long time ago there lived a very special girl named **MARY**.

One day while Mary was in her house **PRAYING** …
… **GOD** sent a messenger to her.

Mary was very surprised to suddenly see someone **STANDING** in front of her. The messenger told her **NOT TO BE AFRAID**.

His name was **GABRIEL**
and …
… he had been sent from
GOD.

The messenger asked Mary to
become the mother of God's
Son, **JESUS**.

Mary said **"YES,"** she would
do what God wanted. She
was excited to know that she
was going to have a baby.

Mary wanted to tell **JOSEPH**, the man that she was going to marry, about the baby.

The **MESSENGER** went to tell Joseph the good news.

What was the messenger from God?
(An angel.)

One Special Night

The Nativity

(Based on Luke 2:1-18, Matthew 2:1-11)

A long, long time ago there lived two very special people. A man named **JOSEPH** ...

... and his wife, **MARY**.

The king of the country in which Mary and Joseph lived wanted to count all the people in his kingdom. Everyone had to go to the city of his grandparents to be counted. It took Mary and Joseph a **LONG, LONG** time to walk all the way to the city of Bethlehem.

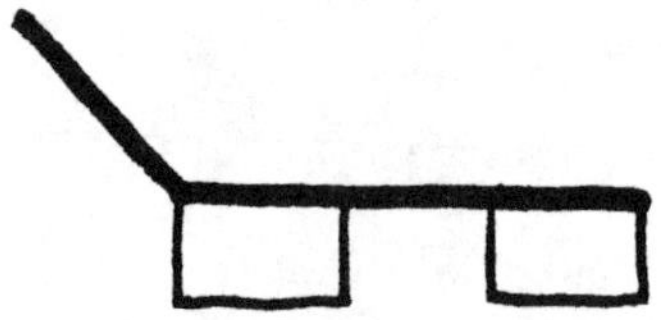

When Mary and Joseph finally got there, they had to find a place to sleep for the night. They **WENT TO AN INN** (like a hotel), but there was no more room.

They went **ALL OVER** the city, but every room was taken.

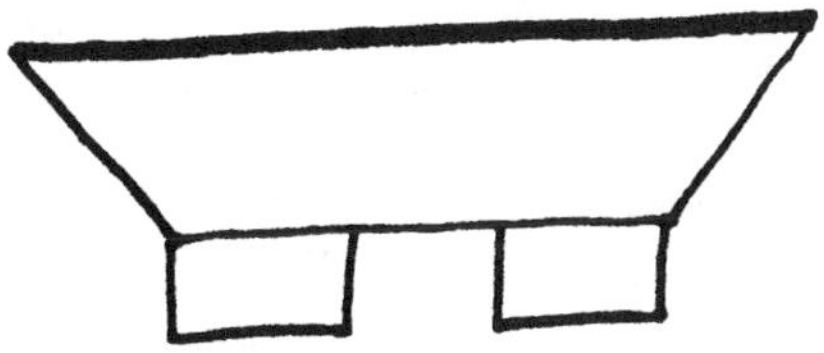

Finally one innkeeper told them that there was a **STABLE AROUND THE BACK** that they could use.

It was warm and dry inside, so Mary and Joseph **WENT IN**①. Inside was a **COW**②...

... and a **DONKEY**. But they were gentle, and Mary and Joseph liked having them there.

Joseph took some **CLEAN, DRY HAY** and made a bed for Mary.

Then he covered her with a **BLANKET**① …
… and took some **HAY**② for himself.

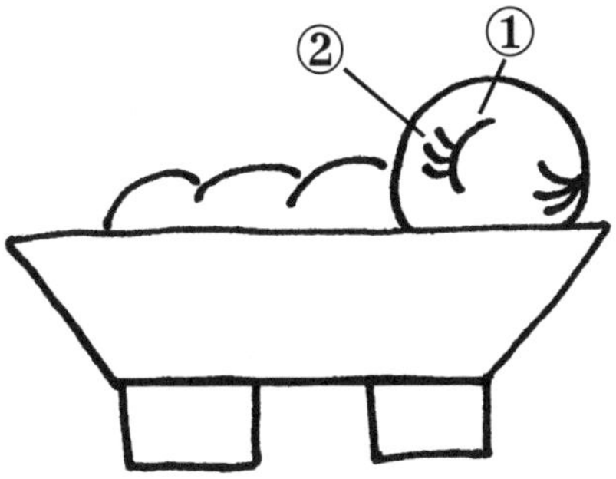

On a **HILLSIDE**① not too far away …
… there were some **SHEPHERDS**② watching their sheep.

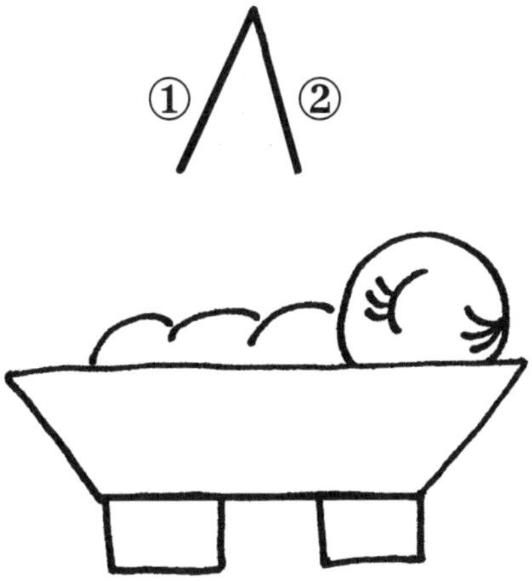

ANGELS told them to hurry to find the stable with Mary and Joseph.

Far away in a different country were some **WISE MEN** who had some very special gifts. They brought gold, frankincense, and myrrh.

Because they lived so far away, the **WISE MEN** needed help to find Bethlehem. God added a beautiful **NEW STAR HIGH IN THE SKY**.

The new star seemed to move, and the Wise Men followed it all the way to Bethlehem.

What did the shepherds and the Wise Men see when they found Mary and Joseph?
(Baby Jesus.)

The Baptism of Jesus

(Based on Luke 3:21-22)

One day **JESUS**① was out walking.

He came by the **RIVER JORDAN**②.

In the river He saw His cousin **JOHN**.

John was bringing people **INTO THE RIVER** and was pouring water over their heads.

John was baptizing the people as a sign that they were part of **GOD'S FAMILY**.

When Jesus saw what John was doing, He **WALKED INTO THE RIVER**.

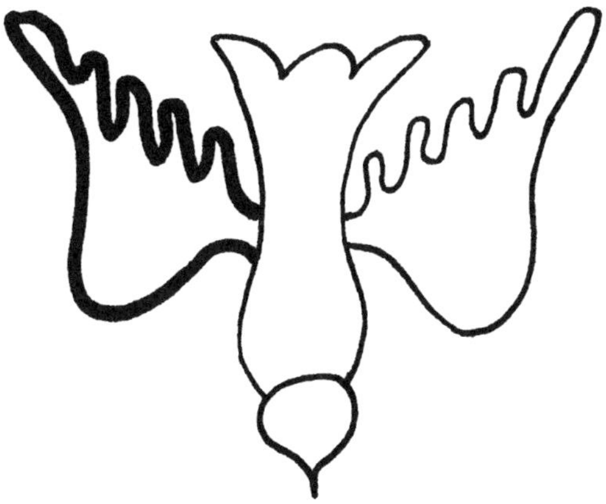

He asked John to **BAPTIZE** Him.

John took some **WATER** and poured it over Jesus. Suddenly they heard a voice from heaven. God said, "This is my Son, who makes me very happy." Then God sent a special sign from the sky.

What did God send?
(The Holy Spirit in the form of a dove.)

The Lilies of the Field

(Based on Matthew 6:26-34)

One day as Jesus was sitting on a **HILLSIDE** ...

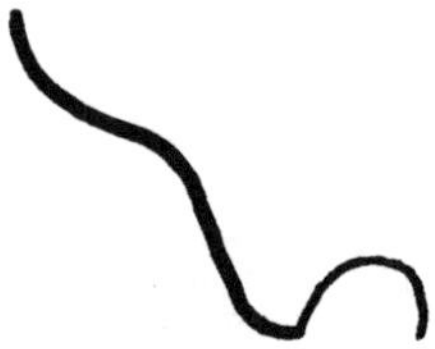

... He told the people to look **AT THE SKY**.

There were many **ANIMALS** flying above.

Jesus told the people that
GOD ...

... **FEEDS** and takes care of
all of them.

They don't worry about a
HOUSE or ...

… **A PLACE TO LIVE**.

Then Jesus said to look around on **THE GROUND**.

He said to see all the beautiful things **GROWING** there.

They don't worry about what **TO WEAR** or ...

... how they **LOOK**.

They are **BEAUTIFUL** because God takes care of them.

Then Jesus said that people are even more important to God our Father than these things. God cares much more for us than any of these.

What did Jesus have the people look at?
(Birds and flowers.)

The Big Storm

(Based on Luke 8:22-25)

One day Jesus was out on **A LAKE** with some of His friends.

Jesus was very tired, so He fell **ASLEEP**.

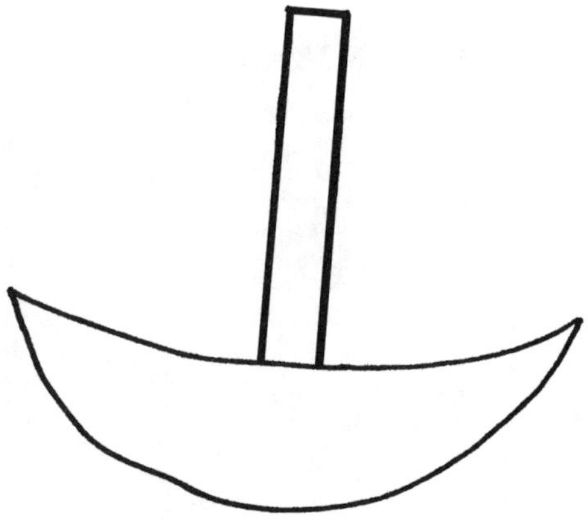

While Jesus was sleeping, a **BIG STORM** came up.

The **WIND BLEW**① …
… and **BIG WAVES**②
splashed water over
everyone.

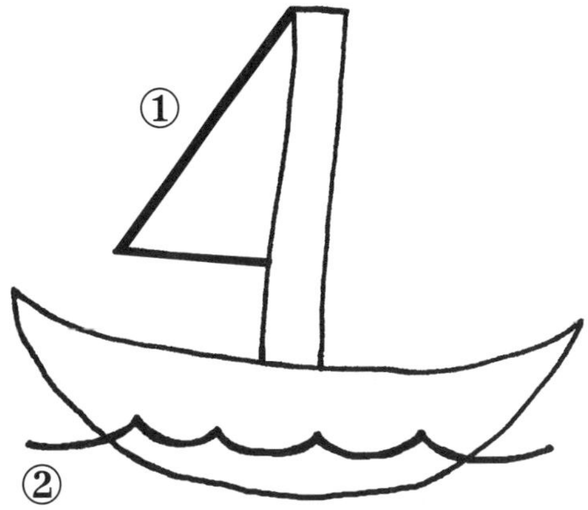

Jesus' friends were very
frightened, so they woke
Jesus up. Jesus stood up and
said, **"BE STILL."**

Suddenly the **WAVES**
CALMED DOWN and the
sea was quiet.

The **SUN** came out again.

Jesus' friends learned they never had to be afraid if they were with Him.

Where was Jesus when He fell asleep?
(In a boat.)

A Feast for All

The Miracle of the Loaves and Fishes
(Based on Mark 6:34-44)

One day Jesus was on a **HILLSIDE** teaching and talking to a lot of people.

There were more than **FIVE THOUSAND** people there.

The people had been listening to **JESUS** all day.

Some of Jesus' friends said that the people were getting very hungry and it was a **LONG WAY** back to town. Jesus wanted to give all the people there something to eat.

He told them to **SIT DOWN**.

The friends of Jesus **LOOKED AND LOOKED** for something to give the people to eat.

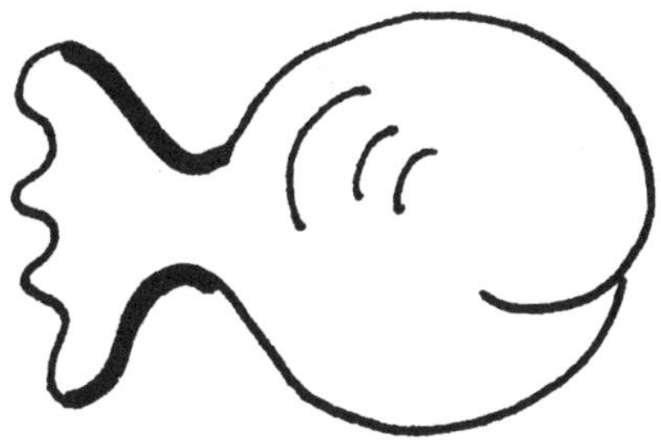

Finally they found a little **BOY** who had some bread and some other food in a little basket.

Jesus blessed the food and told His friends to give it to the people. Every time they took something out of the basket — the **BASKET** was still full.

When all the people ate as much as they wanted, they gathered up all the leftovers and were able to fill up twelve big baskets full of food. Because of Jesus, all those people were able to have enough to eat just from the food the boy had in the little basket.

What else did the boy have in the basket with the loaves of bread?
(Fishes.)

The Good Shepherd

(Based on Luke 15:4-7)

Jesus told His friends a story about a good shepherd:

A shepherd has to watch over a lot of **SHEEP**.

He must take them to the **SWEET GREEN GRASS**① and the **COOL CLEAN WATER**② every day.

At night the shepherd puts all the sheep inside the **SHEEPFOLD** to keep them safe.

A good shepherd knows each sheep and calls them by name. Here's **DOVER** and **BONNIE**.

The sheep **LOVE** the good shepherd.

They know that the shepherd will take care of them. If a **WOLF** tries to hurt the sheep, the shepherd will fight the wolf.

If even one **SHEEP** gets lost, the good shepherd will leave the others …

… and **LOOK AND LOOK** until he finds the lost sheep.

Jesus says that He is the Good Shepherd and He will take very good care of us.

In the story what are we like?
(The sheep.)

The Boy Who Was Sorry

The Prodigal Son

(Based on Luke 15:11-24)

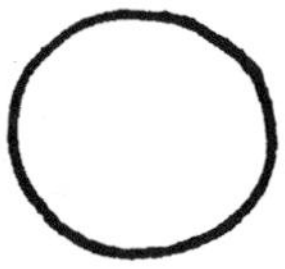

One day Jesus told this story to some people:

Once there was a very rich man who lived in a big **HOUSE**.

This man had **TWO SONS**.

One day the younger son asked for his share of his father's **MONEY**.

The father loved the son, so he gave him the **MONEY**①. The boy took the money and **WENT FAR AWAY**②.

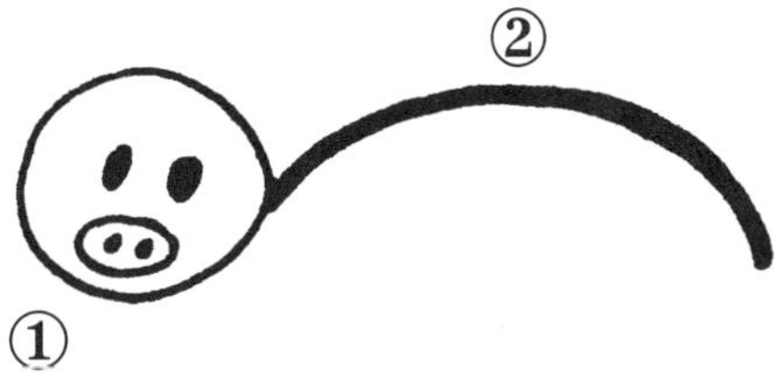

He had **PARTIES** and bought **PRESENTS** for his friends.

Soon all the money was **GONE**.

None of his friends would give him any money or even buy him lunch. He had to get a job feeding animals. Sometimes he was so hungry he ate the animals' **FOOD**.

One day while he was sitting in the mud feeding the animals he thought about **HIS HOME**.

The boy knew that even the people who only worked for his father were treated better and had more to eat than he. He decided **TO GO HOME**.

When his father saw the boy coming far down the road, he ran out to meet him. He was so happy to see his son again that he called all his friends together to have a big party. The boy was very happy that his father still loved him. The boy told his father how sad he felt when he had to feed the animals and eat their food. He said how happy he was to be home and how sorry he was for asking for the money.

What kind of animal did the boy feed?
(A pig.)

Clip Notes

Jesus Heals

(Based on Luke 17:11-19)

One day **JESUS** was walking and talking with His friends.

TEN MEN who were very sick came to talk to Jesus.

They had a sickness that caused their skin to have **SORES ALL OVER** it.

The men knew that **JESUS** had cured many other people.

They asked Jesus to **HELP** them.

Jesus told them to go show themselves **TO THE PRIEST**.

The men turned and started **TO WALK AWAY**.

Suddenly they realized that **ALL THE SORES WERE GONE**. They were very happy!

Most of them ran off happily to go to their **FAMILIES**.

Here is a picture of all those who came back to say "Thank you" to Jesus.

How many men came back to say "Thank you" to Jesus?
(One.)

Clip Notes

Zacchaeus

(Based on Luke 19:1-10)

Once there was a very **SHORT LITTLE MAN** named Zacchaeus.

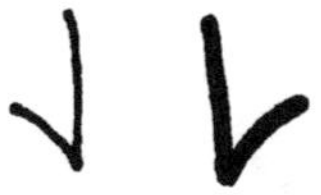

Zacchaeus was a **TAX COLLECTOR**, which meant his job was to collect money from people.

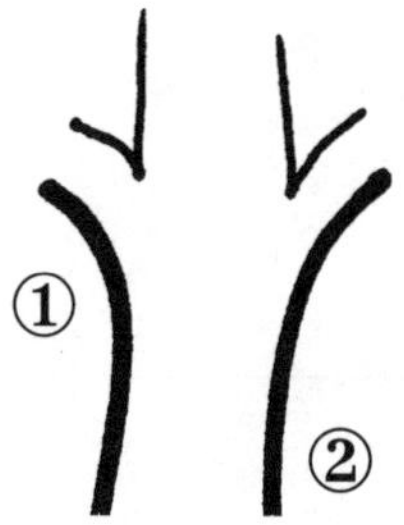

Zacchaeus was not an honest man. If a person owed **TEN DOLLARS**①, Zacchaeus asked for **TWENTY DOLLARS**②...

... and would keep some for himself.

If someone owed **FIFTY DOLLARS**①, Zacchaeus asked for **ONE HUNDRED DOLLARS**② and kept some.

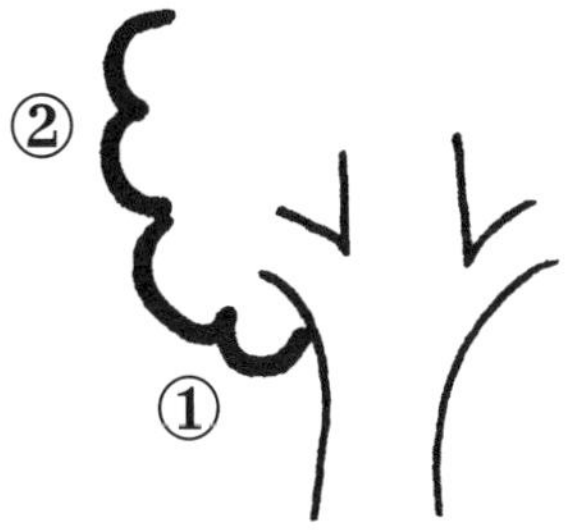

The **PEOPLE** of the city did not like Zacchaeus because he cheated them.

One day Zacchaeus heard that **JESUS** was nearby.

A LOT OF PEOPLE came to see Jesus.

All the people were in front of Zacchaeus and because he was so small he couldn't see. Zacchaeus had to get **HIGHER**.

When Jesus walked by, He **LOOKED UP** and saw Zacchaeus.

Jesus told Zacchaeus to come down. Together they **WENT TO ZACCHAEUS'S** house for dinner.

After Zacchaeus talked to Jesus he became a better person. He gave back the **MONEY** to all the people he cheated. Meeting Jesus changed Zacchaeus.

What did Zacchaeus climb so that he could see Jesus?
(A tree.)

Clip Notes

Jesus and the Children

(Based on Matthew 19:13-15, Luke 18:15-17)

One day Jesus went out to teach the people about **GOD** our Father.

He **WALKED** and **WALKED** all over to see as many people as He could.

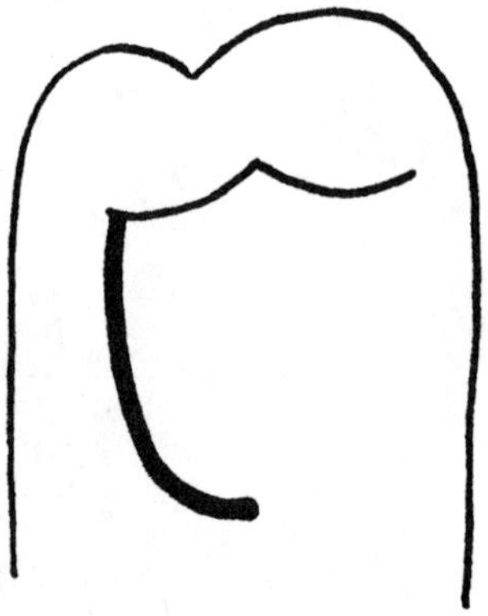

By the end of the day Jesus was **TIRED**.

He found a **TREE** to sit under and lean against.

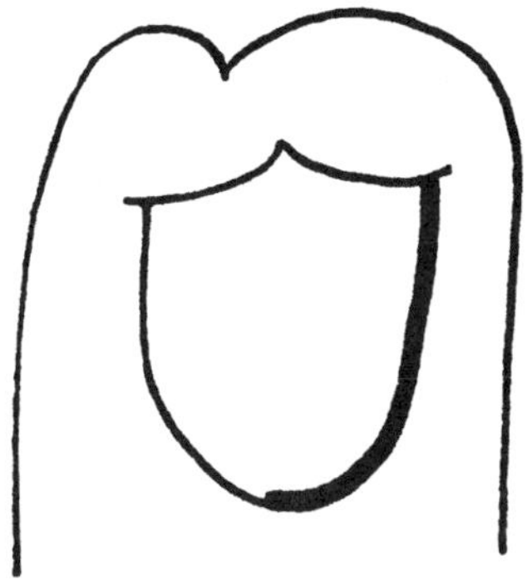

While He rested, some **CHILDREN** came up to Jesus.

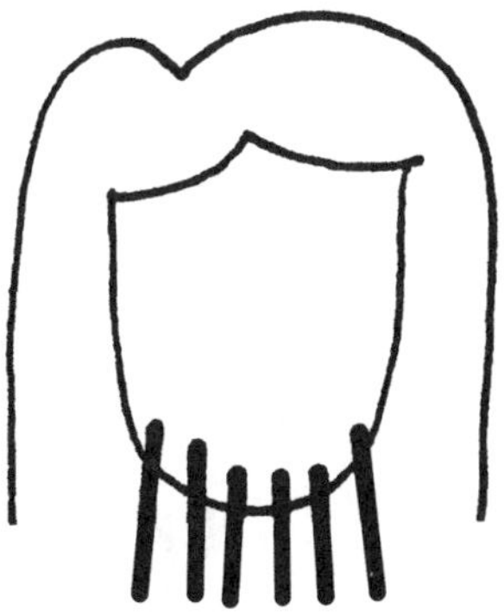

Some of Jesus' **FRIENDS** told the children to leave Jesus alone because He was so tired.

But Jesus said, "Let the **CHILDREN** come to me."

The children **RAN BACK** to Jesus.

Some of them **SAT ON JESUS' LAP** just to be close to Him.

How did Jesus feel about the children coming to Him?
(Happy.)

Clip Notes

The Last Supper

(Based on Luke 22:14-20)

One Thursday evening Jesus and His friends were sitting around **A LONG TABLE** having supper.

His friends were **SAD** because Jesus said He would be leaving them soon.

During the **MEAL** Jesus said a blessing.

Then He **BROKE** the food …

… and **GAVE** it to the others.

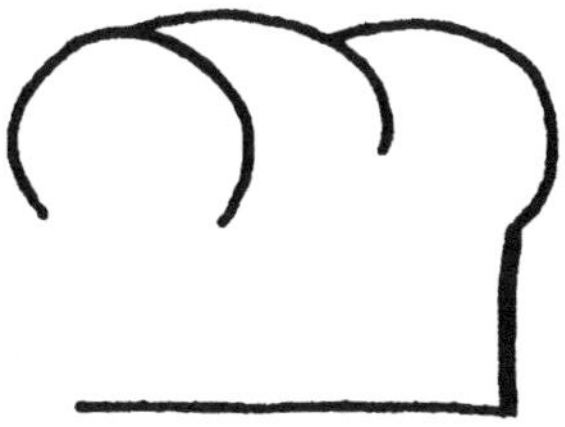

He said, "**THIS IS MY BODY**."

Then **JESUS** ...

... took a **CUP** of wine and blessed it.

He said, "**THIS IS MY BLOOD**."

He **GAVE IT** to His friends.

After they finished, Jesus said, "Do this in remembrance of me."

What did Jesus change into His Body and Blood during this meal?
(Bread and wine.)

This bread and this wine really became Jesus. He did this so that He could stay with His friends always.

Clip Notes

He Is Risen

(Based on Luke 22:14-53, 23:21-56, 24:1-8)

One Thursday evening Jesus met with His friends, the apostles, for supper. They all sat around a **LONG TABLE**. During this supper Jesus gave the apostles their First Communion.

After supper Jesus and the apostles **WENT OUT** into the garden to pray.

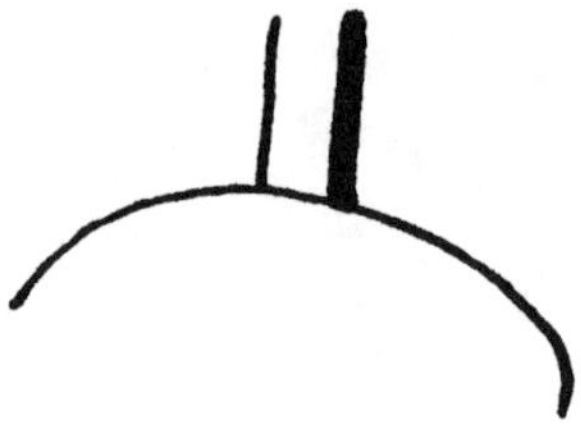

While they were there, some **SOLDIERS** came and took Jesus away to see a man named Pontius Pilate.

Some other **PEOPLE** came
and told lies about Jesus.

PILATE said Jesus must die.

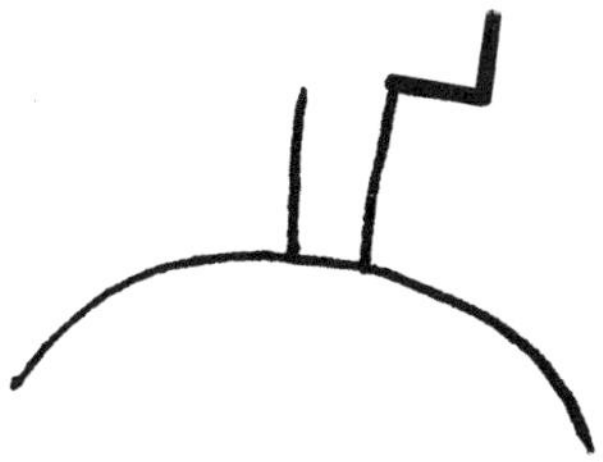

He was taken away and made
to **WALK THROUGH TOWN**
carrying a big heavy cross.

Along the way Jesus fell
THREE TIMES.

When Jesus walked by His mother, **MARY**, she felt very sad to see Him suffering.

Finally they got to the **TOP OF THE HILL** and Jesus was put on the cross. On Friday afternoon Jesus died.

That evening Mary and Jesus' friends put Him in a tomb (something like a cave) and rolled **A BIG STONE** in front of it. All day on Saturday Jesus' friends were very sad because He had died.

Early Sunday morning some of His **FRIENDS** went to visit the tomb. They were very surprised to see that the stone was moved away and Jesus was gone.

An **ANGEL** told them the great news — Jesus was alive again!

Jesus went to visit His mother, Mary, and all His friends. They were happy to know that He was alive. We can be happy too because Jesus is still with us today.

What symbol reminds us that Jesus is alive?
(The empty cross.)

This empty cross can remind us of how Jesus died, was buried, and is alive.

Clip Notes